The Open Gate: A Haiku Journal

For Ruth and Carl
With all best wishes

Jack Greene

The Open Gate: A Haiku Journal

J. C. Greene

iUniverse, Inc.
New York   Lincoln   Shanghai

The Open Gate: A Haiku Journal

Copyright © 2006 by J. C. Greene

All rights reserved. No part of this book may be used or reproduced by any means, graphic, electronic, or mechanical, including photocopying, recording, taping or by any information storage retrieval system without the written permission of the publisher except in the case of brief quotations embodied in critical articles and reviews.

iUniverse books may be ordered through booksellers or by contacting:

iUniverse
2021 Pine Lake Road, Suite 100
Lincoln, NE 68512
www.iuniverse.com
1-800-Authors (1-800-288-4677)

Cover photo credit: "The South Gate" in the Morikami Japanese Gardens. Photo courtesy of the Morikami Museum and Japanese Gardens, Delray Beach, Florida, with special thanks to Kristina Schmidt.

ISBN-13: 978-0-595-40895-5 (pbk)
ISBN-13: 978-0-595-85258-1 (ebk)
ISBN-10: 0-595-40895-8 (pbk)
ISBN-10: 0-595-85258-0 (ebk)

Printed in the United States of America

Contents

Introduction .... *vii*

Part I—Up to Age 70 .... *1*

Part II—After Age 70 .... *99*

About the Author *119*

Introduction

In *The Open Gate: A Haiku Journal*, I have used modern Haiku to describe some of my experiences and perceptions during the past 78 years. What is a Haiku, and what are the differences between classical Japanese Haiku and modern Haiku?

Classical Japanese Haiku are short poems consisting of only three lines, containing neither rhyme nor rhythm, that are arranged in five, seven, and five syllables (a total of only 17 syllables). Typically, a season reference is included, adjectives are discouraged, and the Haiku should be true to feeling, not conceptual, and devoid of ego. Gilbert Highet, renowned author, scholar, and professor, described good Haiku as being "deceptively simple." And Basho, the acknowledged 17th century master of Japanese Haiku, reputedly said that if one is able to produce even a few good Haiku in a lifetime, that is enough.

Some years ago Japan Air Lines ran a contest for Haiku written in English and received an astonishing response of about 40,000 individual entries, of which only 200 were judged suitable for publication. Evidently, writing Haiku is quite popular and writing good Haiku remains difficult.

What accounts for the popularity of Haiku in English, and in many other languages as well? For one thing, writers of modern Haiku tend to view the strict rules for classical Haiku as goals rather than constraints. For another, especially in western countries, greater freedom of expression allows for the direct expression of feelings rather than having to mask them as Nature experiences. I believe such innovations are in keeping with Basho's dictum, "I do not seek to follow in the footsteps of the men of old, I seek the things they sought." And Oscar Wilde's wonderful description of a beautiful form would certainly include modern Haiku: "The singular characteristic of a beautiful form is that one can put into it whatever one wishes, and see in it whatever one chooses to see. It is Beauty that makes the reader a creator in turn, and whispers of a thousand different things not present in the mind of its creator."

I started this Haiku journal at age 55. The first 11 poems in Part I are recollections, in chronological order, of much earlier events. The remaining poems were written largely as events occurred, except for a few that I was unable to write until years later.

Some poems acknowledge the enduring influence on me of various well-known writers, poets, composers, and artists, and some poems are dedicated to special friends including Jim Craib, Walter Landauer, Bill Hess, Ken Siegel, and Saeko Ogasawara. Among the family members referred to are my son Dan, who died of cancer at age 29, and my uncle "J.P.," with whom I lived for eight years. He was one of the last survivors of the rightly famous and much lauded "Lost Battalion" of World War I.

The division of this journal into Parts I and II at age 70 is indicative of the sea change in me at that time caused by my own bout with cancer.

I encourage everyone to keep a Haiku journal. Writing Haiku is fun and also an enriching experience that can lead to increased self-knowledge and greater powers to intuit feelings and to describe them succinctly, all of which lead to better Haiku. As for other "rewards," the answer is best given by Emily Dickinson:

"Fame is a bee.

It has a song—

It has a sting—

Ah, too, it has a wing."

I would like to thank Saeko Ogasawara for her critical reading of some early poems and for her insight and helpful suggestions. Special thanks are due to my wife, Felice, for carefully reading all the poems and her encouragement and support during the numerous occasions when I was distracted while composing Haiku. Thanks also to Donna, without whose help this book would not have been published.

The Open Gate: A Haiku Journal is dedicated to my sons Jon and Andy, and my grandchildren Sarah, Jeremy, Alex, and Zoe, who at age 10 had already written some wonderful Haiku. She realized early that Haiku are slippery critters that are difficult to catch and require much grooming before presentation.

Part I—Up to Age 70

"The unexamined life is not worth living."
—*Socrates*

"I do not seek to follow in the footsteps of the men of old, I seek the things they sought."
—*Basho*

"Look within—the secret is inside you."
—*Hui-Neng*

"We must endure our going hence as our coming hither—ripeness is all."
—*Shakespeare*

"Rem Tene, Verba Sequentur."
(Grasp the thing, words will follow.)
—*Cato (The Elder)*

○

Mystic presences—
An old tree and flowers
Their masks withdrawn.
—
Age 5.

○

The storm just over
Sunset lights only the tall tree's top
Where a robin sings.
—
Age 6.

○

The pond at sunset—
Night sounds replace day sounds
As the light fades.
—
Age 8.

○

Father's hand guides mine
Identifying stars in the sky—
And a direction for me.
—
Age 8.

○

○

Grandfather
Sits alone reading Sabbath prayers—
No wink today.

○

Grandmother
Lights the Sabbath candles
Her face already aglow.

○

Arriving home late
Feet wet, face frostbitten, she smiles—
Smell of spice.
—
For Aunt Rachel.

○

In the green tree's shade
The first yellow leaf slowly falls
Into Autumn's outstretched hand.

○

Stretched between two trees
A spider web blocks the path—
Not caught, yet captured.

○

○

An Autumn wind—
From the unused sandbox
A tin cup rolls away.

○

On the lotus pad
A dragonfly slowly lands—
All town sounds recede.

○

Spring day—
Still, hang the leash and collar;
I empty the food bowl.
—
Guri's death.

○

Wheelchair bound he sits
Looking through the hall windows—
Sunshine on the floor.
—
For J.P.

○

○

Leaving the hospital
He sits upright in his wheel chair—
A one-day pass.

Returning that night
Through dark, deserted halls I wheel him—
We fall silent.

—

For J.P.

○

A collection box
For disabled heroes of the last war—
Empty.

○

Shakespeare read aloud—
The retired schoolteacher
Alone in her room.

—

For Aunt Esther.

○

○

Cloudy afternoon—
Into the empty bird nest
Autumn leaves falling.

—

Mom's death.

○

Old, crippled soldier—
Now taken down at twilight
The flag raised at dawn.

—

J.P.'s death.

○

A fair, young soldier
Mourning his fallen comrade—
Statue in the rain.

○

The bronze vase
Filled with summer flowers and cool water
Begins to weep.

○

○

Victors

Leaving prayers of thanks
The victors removed their stones
Little changing the pile.

Fallen

A crude memorial
Left by their death-stilled hands—
Only the wind moaned.

Visitors

The stark pile
Is embellished by the silence
Of its visitors.

———

Viking/Saxon battlesite in the Lake District, England. Each warrior placed a stone on a pile before battle. Afterward, the survivors each removed one stone.

○

Upon captor's clay
Kneaded with a captive's tears
A solitary pine tree.

———

Karatsu pottery.

○

○

One crow, explaining
Is rebutted by another—then all the others
In a cacophony of chaos!

○

Wealth and fame are tasty
But one's appetite increases—
In the peach tree, birds sing.

Searching for the way
Past fading, future clouded—
In the breeze, flowers dance.

Thirsty no longer
Bottomless well water—ah—
Ice melts, the pond deepens.

○

A sudden wind—
The colorful oak leaves drop
On the feeding roots.

○

Partly cloudy day—
Intermittently entering the dark woods
Rays of golden light.

○

○

More than hot water
The hands of the tea master
Warm the cold tea bowl.
—
For Saeko.

○

Quietly the sea recedes
Taking with it
Something of me.

○

Hidden
Amongst Autumn's colors
One green leaf.

○

The spider
Its web completed
Contracts—and waits.

○

A shooting star
Attracts all eyes
Leaving them aglow in darkness.

○

○

The white moth
Lands on a white Vinca
Then disappears!

○

Options rejected
Seemingly unconnected
Form the path—not taken.

○

A solitary pine tree
Dignified and full of grace—
Nature reflects Kenzan's face.

○

Early sunlight
Enters the walled church garden—
Outside, rush hour starts.

○

In the driving rain
The flowering cherry tree
Releases a petal shower.

○

○

The notes of the flute
Settle on the peach blossoms—
Heavy, they drift down.

○

In the old stone garden
A crow lands on the thick moss—
Unbroken silence.

○

The snow falls
On the muted notes
Of a distant flute.

○

Transforming music
Falling on attentive ears—
Blossoms from this rain.

○

Transforming music—
The mirror of understanding is cleansed
Tear by tear.

○

○

Bent down by ripe fruit—
Bearing the heavy burden
Without breaking.

When the fruit is gone
The branch still droops somewhat—
Final remembrance.

—

For Saeko on the death of her mother.

○

The thorn withdrawn
Healing then begins—
Unlike sharp words.

○

Topped by thick clouds
The peaks and the paths to them—
Unseen, the sun.

○

Always changing
The waves catch our attention—
Below, the still depths.

○

○

Dwarfed and twisted
To suit man's aesthetics—
Yet, it flowers.

○

On a lonely road
While walking slowly—time stopped—
Only this moment.

○

Autumn leaves
Laden with pain
Sailing away.

○

Grief
Overflowing
Rolls down my cheeks.

○

Guitar in hand
He sang to heaven
An unfinished song.
—
Dan's death.

○

○

Heavy rain
Preparing his death bed
Heavy rain.

Drifting slowly
Into the black whirlpool
Infrequent beams of light.

In the black swirl
Grasping for a way out
Until drawn under.

○

Not submerged by waves
Of memories and dreams—
A rare moment.

○

Downward they spiral
To join Autumn's Danse Macabre
Brightly dressed at last.

Wind stirred
Like colorful Dervishes
They whirl in circles.

Stopping short they fall
Forming a patchwork quilt
That warms the cold earth.

○

○

By moonlight
Only the Japanese maple glows—
In the night, leaves fall.

○

Much or too little
And grieving is criticized—
Freely, my heart bleeds.

○

His achievements
Then criticized as imperfect
Now gladden my heart.

○

When the seed of love
Sprouts in the soil of acceptance
Wholesome is the fruit.

When sprouted late
From the soil of anguish
Remorse is the fruit.

○

○

Knowledge and truth
In criticism's garden
Go hand in hand.

Planted in the shade
Caressed by the dry breeze
Love's flower withers.

After a hard rain
Away washed criticism—
White blooms love's flower.

○

Without explaining
When asked my children's number
I still reply "three."

○

Rootless
The log sprouts leaves of flame
Consuming itself.

○

Through pain's screen revealed—
Society's nakedness
And Nature's grandeur.

○

○

Self exploring
At dawn they play apart
A boy and a girl.

Coming together
Each finds fulfillment
In noon's brightness.

Evening—
Society her trumpet
The spirit, his.

○

Symbol of his hope—
Not the strange red blossom
But the many buds.
—
For Dan.

○

A lifetime's treasures
In an old cardboard box—
Missing is love.

○

○

From now quiet rooms
Grown children carry away
Memorabilia.

○

The young girl
Stoops to pluck a flower
Now in her shadow.

○

The elixir
Squeezed from the press of life:
A few drops of love.

Given away
The supply increases
Taken, no surfeit.

Sweet in remembrance
Or in anticipation
Sweeter yet, now.

○

Falling
Through the quiet
One acorn.
—
For Siegfried Sassoon.

○

○

Joining the breeze
The sapling sways and twists
In a Pas de Deux.

○

Hollowed by flames—
Steps ascending to another road
Leading elsewhere.

○

Children's voices
Carried by the wind—
Echoes from my heart.

○

From boys
War makes old men
And young corpses.

○

Army buddies—
First, hesitating, they learn trust
And at the end, love.

○

○

Reaching
Across seventy years
The cold hand of terror.
—

For J.P., Co. I, 307 Inf., 77 Div., AEF;
Member of The Lost Battalion.

○

While others searched
For joy and contentment
He found them daily.

○

In the pool
A young boy plays with his father—
Watching them, an old man.

○

In its quiet eddies
Float the treasures
Of life.

○

○

Removed by time and pain
Layer upon layer of partial perception
Revealing reality whole.

A shining young boy
Dressed in jacket and bow tie
Sings, happy and smiling.

Present again
Undiminished by time or me
The song and the singer.

○

Ripeness
Unfolds the bud
Of understanding.

○

The birds
As the rain begins to fall
Stop singing.

○

Natural temple
Inaccessible part of a rugged mountain—
Empty—except for one spirit.

○

○

The latest of many
Yet the glow is different—
First memorial candle for Dan.

○

From years past
Come the joys of this Autumn—
Cold blows Winter's early wind.

○

Like fruit on a tree
Hang the experiences of life
Slowly ripening.

The child
Attracted by its colors
Cannot reach the fruit.

The adolescent
Aware of the fruit
Ignores it.

The adult
Drawn to the juiciest fruit
Picks some.

Old people
Finally ripe as the fruit
Simply digest it.

○

○

This day
The landscape tended for years
Is strangely different.

Gone suddenly
The incremental changes of yesterdays
The seeming static presence.

A starting point
Seen now as by a new owner
Peering from the future.

○

All doors open
As the locks are sprung by Death
Releasing captive feelings.

Near day's end
All feelings return to but one cell
Most changed, none independent.

○

Bent down by ripe fruit
The branch bears the heavy burden
Then snaps.

○

○

From beginning to end
Stretches a lifeline of stability
On the journey called life.

Some there are
Who travel line in hand
Faces calm, eyes aglow.

Letting go of the line
Some seek thrills each moment
Faces flush, eyes restless.

Some wander in many directions
Alternately leaving, then regaining the line
Faces bittersweet, eyes focused.

○

A cold wind
Blows the door shut—
Restlessness on both sides.

○

Swift messenger
Delivering and taking simultaneously—
Red-splotch calling card.

○

○

Whatever
The unfolding pace of the weather
In step ripens the fruit.

For nature's pests
Devouring sooner rather than later
Partly ripe is sufficient.

Of ripening
This nibbling too is a part—
Seeds fall to the ground.

○

Flower of an hour
With much, and little
In thy power.

○

Innocently, the plant thrives
A secret poison held inside—
Devourers only may imbibe.

○

Yesterday's raging torrent
On today's flower-spotted desert
Is a stagnant puddle.

○

○

A child
Leading a parade
With no followers.

○

At dawn's stealthy approach
One bird sings tentative greetings—
Awakening a crescendo of certainty.

○

This gladness
Opens the wound of sadness—
On Father's Day, two calls.

○

From the ocean of time
A wave of joy returns—
Song of a hidden bird.

○

A haze
Of fragmented facts
Hiding wonder.

○

○

Atop the pedestal
Of deep feelings
The lens of clear vision.

○

A deserted cottage
By lush vines overgrown—
Sound of a wind chime.

○

To greet this dawn
Only the plaintive song
Of the mourning dove.

○

From the wall
As rain begins to fall
Their names vanish.
—
Vietnam Veterans Memorial, Washington, D.C.

○

The robin
Annoyed by Mozart's music
Cocks his head in vain.

○

○

The woodcutter
Wielding speech and axe alike
Quickly reaches the point.

○

Death
The hooded figure that stands apart
Approaches silently.

A brief ceremony—
After the ritual exchange
He carries life away.

Under a living roof
Supported by living columns
He feasts.

○

Specimen in a museum showcase
A beautiful bird, now extinct—
The room empty, shades drawn.

○

Reading names on the wall
The grieving see their reflections—
Reflecting the names, their tears.
—
Vietnam Veterans Memorial, Washington, D.C.

○

○

On this birthday
Flowers he planted now cover the hill—
Yet he grows no older.
—
For Dan.

○

By moonlight
The first frost tenderly embraces
Each remaining flower.

○

In the sky
Statues atop the wall
Peer into infinity.

○

In warm Autumn sunshine
Around a deserted well
The last flowers ripen.

○

Autumn—
Quietly, leaf by leaf
The cover deepens.

○

○

All deep emotions
Tear by tear, overflow the well—
The mask reveals the source.

○

Walking again
By the seashore of youth—
Footprints vanish, the wind cold.

○

An obstacle encountered
In pursuing the possible
Nature zigzags.

○

Trapped
The trickle rises
Finding an outlet.

○

Summer's end—
Death tints the weak growth
While Autumn colors the rest.

○

○

Again and again
The fly bumps the windowpane—
A rear turn freedom attains.

○

The poet
Now letting no feelings out.
Invites Nature in.

The soil depleted
Prose struggles
Where poetry bloomed.

―

Vol. II of Thoreau's Journals.

○

Sitting quietly side by side
Aware of each other's awareness
In a summer garden.

○

Spring—
Yet, the season
Is the beholder's.

○

○

He requests sherry while dying—
An ordinary glass she offers;
"Crystal," his soft reply.

○

Nature unfolds—
In each production's portion of eternity
Uncertainty continues.

○

I threw my watch away—
Now, my time and Nature's time
Always rhyme.

○

Rounding a turn
A tangential escape I suddenly imagined
And found the timeless world.

A start, but no beginning
A finish, but no end
Aware of being aware—now.

○

Gone the leafy cloak—
Bare gray limbs with icy skins
Wearing tufts of snow.

○

○

Gashes
From which hot venom spewed
Steadily bleed remorse.

For newer wounds
Though it starts the same
Before it spews, congeals.

○

"He's gone west"
Of the dead it was said—
There, the sun sets.

Gone now the last—
In the west, "Assembly" sounds
For the final roll call.

—

For the Lost Battalion.

○

Psychic balm
For pain held interior:
Loving metaphors exterior.

○

○

Of all poets
The auburn-haired maiden clad in white
Alone shames me to silence.

Beneath freckles, honesty
And a soul with exquisite sensitivity
Transmuting feelings into gold.

—

For Emily Dickinson.

○

Time nor grief bring relief—
From pain, understanding—and then remorse
So pain spreads, remorse fed.

At season's end
Understanding may swallow remorse
Leaving such an empty place.

Or
Remorse may swallow understanding—
Its place, death takes.

○

○

The grandiose order[†]—fulfilled—
For each alive, two had died
Holding the gut-strewn prize.

Beneath praise piled high
Misgivings continued to smoulder—
A paltry, costly prize.

For loved lives lost
Also came repeated blame—
Silence, the reply.

Quietly, doubt's fire ignited
Precluding redemptive love from sprouting
Then spread, by remorse fed.

Uncontrollably it raged
Until quenched in the great salt sea—
The grandiose order—fulfilled.

For Col. Charles W. Whittlesey (1883–1921), Commander of the Lost Battalion on the anniversary of his suicide by drowning.

[†] Advance "without regard of losses and without regard to the exposed conditions of the flanks…"
             —Gen. John J. Pershing.

○

○

Only the boundary
May the living know
Of heaven's territory.

Over the boundary
A leap of faith to the interior—
Uncertainty alone may return.

Those who leap not
An interior deserted surmise
And note uncertainty's every return.

○

How taste the wine divine
That comes but once a life—
Unknowing, gulp it down?

○

Young eyes
Take its every measure
And read its poetry too.

The same object
Older eyes careless see
Evoking only memories.

○

○

Feelings
Seeking light
Cast poetic shadows.

○

Not perceived of Moment
While each is yet alive
Life's moments simply die.

At twilight, if ever
Some may resurrected be
In reverie.

Perceived of Moment
While each is yet alive
Life's moments live, not die.

○

A many-petaled flower
Lacking fragrance in any weather:
Words with logic strung together.

So, sparingly were used
The words at his command;
His face made you understand.

○

○

Putting the world down
At a steady pace I walked away
To the steep-sloped mountain.

Astonished derision—
"Why renounce a vibrant life?"
Ask dwellers on the plain.

A constant struggle it is
To climb and not come down—
Increasingly wonderful the view.

○

Time unwraps his final gifts—
In every loved one yet alive
Love multiplies.

○

The cardinal flies away
Leaving behind a petal shower
And silence.

○

From the flower
Of paradox
The scent of truth.
—
For Thoreau and Oscar Wilde.

○

○

Slowly, Death's cold finger
Points out every weakness
In the relationship.

○

Dispelled by the rising sun
The morning shadows gladly go—
At dusk, ominously, they regather.

○

The struggle completed
Nature stands in silent prayer
As Autumn approaches.
—
For Wilfred Owen.

○

Self-excoriation's reason:
Upon the golden shelf
Much plated ware.

○

Inebriate all senses—
Leaning against the flowering tree
Rapture engulfs me.
—
For Thoreau and Emily Dickinson.

○

○

In the crosshairs
Of essence and detail
The target of understanding.

○

In desolation, wild asters
Blooming when all else has faded—
Outpost of loveliness.

○

Before taking the gift
Death serves a tasteless meal
On broken china.

○

In the darkness
Sounds of rain
And one mourning dove.

○

The favorite plate
Of the red-haired, blue-eyed curator:
Red and blue Chun ware.

○

○

Not of the center
At the perimeter I chose to dwell
Different and disdainful.

A lonely spot—
Desire rejected virtue became
Reinforcing disdain.

○

The sword—
Whose hand its hilt shall take
Must ancient decisions remake.

○

Pain is the screen
Through which truth
Can be seen.

○

This day
The past nibbled steadily
On the present.

○

Birdsong—
The intended, a cat, and I
Head toward the tree.

○

○

Suddenly
This moment is not my present
And eternity breaks through.

○

The overcast Autumn sky
Fills the bare forest
With a mysterious gloom.

○

Deep into time
My anchor roots tunnel
Yet, one cut, I sway.
—
For Jim Craib.

○

Seeds of hope
Land on the ashes of destruction—
The unexpected sprouts.

○

Through the mirror
To the world behind the world—
Alive—but detached.

○

○

The poetry shelf—
One book whispers
"Do not let me die."
———
For Edna St. Vincent Millay.

○

Snowstorm—
Alone I trudge past closed shops
Down the quiet street.

○

Forgotten memories—
The one recalled
Brings companions.

○

Turned upon itself
The bright light winces
While revealing its sources.

○

Surrounded
By thorns of pain
World without the world.

○

○

Sunrise—
In the deserted playground
The breeze lifts one swing.

○

From the treetop
Snowdust falls
Golden in the sunlight.

○

The cancer
That devoured his body
Also ate my heart.

○

Pain
Tears off each bud in the garden
Day after day.

○

Today
The past
Drifted away.

○

○

Growth—
Plants have sun and rain
Man, pleasure and pain.

○

Severe winter storm—
May the fragile chirps
Become melodies next spring.

○

Birdsong
Penetrates the barrier—
Life—surrounded by bliss.

○

Carved, this face
By pleasure, pain, wind, and rain—
And long thoughts.

○

In the void
Left by self given away
Union blossoms.

○

○

Hurricane-driven waves
Submerge the huge rocks—
Quietly, they reappear.

○

Prelude

In a front-line trench
All listen to the foreboding whistle—
A direct hit!

Finale

Abandoned
This small farm village—
Only a cenotaph remains.

○

The open front door
Seen against the bare wall—
As on the last day.

○

Autumn twilight—
As a breeze stirs
The first leaves fall.

○

○

A hawk circles overhead
Its shadow racing along the ground
Chased by a puppy.

○

A boy's homemade bow
Launched one strange arrow
That led him through time.

○

Left alone on earth
Would today be like your death
Or birth?

○

With each caress
The bee gathers pollen
And the flower conceives.

○

Loneliness is the black bird
That steals the seeds of joy
From the flower of life.

○

○

A sudden breeze
Delivers a gift taken from the honeysuckle
And continues on.

○

From the temple of despair
Ascends black smoke that rides the air
Seeking those who truly care.

○

Describing anything
I also describe
Myself.

○

Cello strokes—
My heart soars
On breezes of yesterday.

Visions
Perceived then, since held tight
Seen, now, in softer light.

When Nature
Becomes my nature
Everywhere, such light shines.

○

○

Toward sunrise flies the crow—
Its shadow heads west
Where the sun sets.

○

Death
Requires neither auditions nor rehearsals—
Yet, who is prepared?
—
For Edmond.

○

Poignant, the performance
When the part played
Was himself.
—
For Edmond.

○

In this slant of light
Only dead trees, like ghosts,
Show white.

○

All scenes
I search
For dreams.

○

○

Terrible, the swish
Of tear-wetted silk
Cut by a sword.

○

A flowering dogwood tree—
In this assembly of joy
One Buddha-like blossom.

○

All night long
Fragrances from rain
Breaking the drought.

○

A Blue Jay's call—
Its business
Always urgent.

○

For lack of Love
A soul may die—
Settle not, nor lie.

○

○

While each mind
Hosts a universe
Each soul waits alone.

○

In the voice
Of this wind of Autumn
The loneliness inside a tomb.

○

The shadow
Of a praying mantis—
Its owner unseen.

○

Deep, this lake—
The wind only ripples
Its serenity.

○

Laughable—yet touching—
A nightingale and a frog
Each singing with conviction.

○

○

The feeling
Where loneliness or sorrow dwelled
Remains contagious.

Where joy dwelled
The feeling is of one golden moment
Frozen in time.

○

To an ideal youth
A perpetual moment of radiance
From the chisel of love.
—
The statue "Youth of Marathon" in the Athens
 National Museum.

○

Autumn—
Moonlight enters
The closed shop.

○

Saying no
By describing the limitations
On Yes.

○

○

Athens—
Marble dust
On my shoes.

Spring's extraordinary blossom
Lies desiccated in summer dust
Its seed destroyed.

Yet, at Delphi
Where prophecy dwelled
A purple wild flower blooms.

○

Breached, the wall
By the softness
Of treachery.

○

Most anchor
In the warm sea
Of mediocrity.

On the distant shore
A tall grass plume shows
Where the cool wind goes.

○

○

Dawn—
Spring dances
And sings.

Noon—
Summer stretches
Then slumbers.

Afternoon—
Autumn halts
Then falls.

Evening—
Winter sits
And shivers.

○

Splattered with blood
The heavy gate drops
With a terrible thud.

○

In the cold Autumn wind
Only one praying mantis
Watches over the cocoon.

○

○

Of many homes, one:
The spiritual orphanage
By Nature run.

○

Out of the darkness
Comes a throttled cry—
Victim, fox, and death nearby.

○

The cloud of the day
By the wing of Death
Was brushed away.
—

For Walter Landauer.

○

Coaxed by unusual weather
The plant offers untimely
Its floral treasure.

○

Notes are released
From the harpsichord's heart
Like sparks in the dark.

○

○

Near the monks' quarters
A tomato plant grows
In a begging bowl.

○

Above the edge
The black sky is filled
With unknown stars.

○

Infinity enumerated
Minus One and one—
Buddha's unique sum.

○

Grace is said
Yet, tastiness finally dispels
Thoughts about killing.

○

This day, sensed the last
His feeble hand clutches
The bridge to the past.
—
My last visit with J.P.

○

○

In the city of sorrow
None welcome
Tomorrow.

In the city of joy
Oh
Boy!

In the city between
Only masks
Are seen.

○

In love's breeze
A day that would smoulder
Burns brightly.

○

Measured by the handful
The dark sea is clear
The blue sky invisible.

○

Loneliness
Exists in solitude and in crowds
Blocking light like a cloud.

○

○

Death watches impartially
As the fox hunts
In deep snow.

○

This day:
A lead sword
With a dull edge.

○

My eyes wrote checks
For flowers blue and flowers brown—
My heart cashed one.

Shame dwells in shadow—
Yet, the light of truth
Finds and sears the heart.

○

One by one
The echoes
Diminish.

○

Colorless—
The role played
Became life.

○

○

During solitude
Comes the inarticulate guest
Such as ecstasy, or regret.

○

Loneliness
Is love that finds no home
Or one standing on regret.

○

Since understanding is absent
Experience chooses for its partner
The butterfly of illusion.

○

Colors that describe
Passionate brush strokes that interpret;
This painting whispers poetry.†

Colors that make soft notes
Outlines that make soft chords;
This painting hums music.‡

---

† For Van Gogh (and Basho).
‡ For Monet (and Debussy).

○

○

The moon lies seductively
On a blanket of wild flowers
Under the stars.
―
For Baudelaire.

○

A dream that would flower
But yields fruit eaten by pain
Gives despair a darker name.

○

No dream
Suspended in the past
Lives again, recast.

○

Arriving last
Comes the great sadness
Bearing no pain.

○

To die
Unripened
Is the only defeat.

○

○

Exuberant staccato—
The trumpet sings
With a throat of joy.

Languorous legato—
The trumpet sighs
With a throat of sorrow.

○

The empty boat
Tossed by wind and wave
Rights itself, repeatedly.

○

Nature, frowning, has its way
Upsetting the garden's composure
Every day.

○

The final "poem":
A cry from the heart
That penetrated stone.
—
For Rimbaud.

○

○

The mixed colors comprising reality
Scattered by the prism of perception
Go separate monochromatic ways.

○

The winged seed's dilemma:
Drop into the soil of the past
Or await the next breeze?

○

No breeze stirs
And all is silent
As the sun rises.

A beautiful day—
Distance and time
Drift away.

○

A light rain—
The dry stream bed
Glistens.

○

Appearing randomly
Flowers from the Past and the Future
Dot the path of Now.

○

○

The open gate
For no apparent reason
Closes halfway.

○

Life
Hums haunting melodies
Seldom overheard.

○

The soul
Unfolds
Petal by petal.

○

The tree of Solitude
Has roots in the earth's heart
And no dead branches.

The tree of Loneliness
Has roots in a dry stream bed
And withered leaves.

Heavy with fruit
The hybrid tree of Solitude and Loneliness
Is unvisited.

○

○

Deeper feelings:
To love pink tea roses
And not describe them.
—
For Andre Gide.

○

From a distance, the Parthenon
Its glory restored
By the moonlight.

○

To each seed
Nature gives an entire past
And three possible futures.

○

As the heavy door closes
Sighs of resignation from one hinge
Groans of reluctance from another.

○

The caterpillar
Becomes a butterfly—
A boy tries.

○

○

Afraid to try
The fledgling finally leaps
And flies

○

In the hurricane's eye
The battered ship floats becalmed
Its destination—gone.

○

The cicada
Chants an insistent invitation
For Autumn's return.

Autumn arrives—
Relentlessly, the weakening cicada pleads
"Mate, before I die."

○

In the meadow
Creeping shadows
Steal sunset's gilding.

○

A gift
From the departing birds of summer:
Silent days for ripening.

○

○

In the darkness
Two hoot owls discuss strategy
In an ancient Morse code.

○

Those who reach
The realm of mysticism
Arrive with Nothing.

○

Constant change seeking Perfection
Is this Nature's eternal plan?
Alas, the chaos vexes man.

○

In the everlasting change
Of the indifferent sea
Seagulls bob calmly.

○

Unexcited by Spring's caresses
Buds on this tree do not swell—
Forever, Winter's touch will tell.

○

○

The old woman becomes lively
As she tells her old stories
To a new listener.

○

The artist
Finally paints from the heart—
These pictures stand apart.

○

Snowstorm—
The solitude
Also deepens.

○

The different worlds
On each side of the window
Are both made of thoughts.

○

Desire supposes a future
Its denial prolongs the past
Beyond both, Now that lasts.

○

○

The composer
Who fled the farm when young
Writes nostalgic music.

○

Both see
The same things—
One sighs, one sings.

○

External lights
Taken in
Turn soonest dim.

Internal lights
Sent out
Cast shadows of doubt.

○

In the frozen silence
As the first snow begins to fall
A crow searches the lawn.

○

The wind sings—
Then leaves
On silent wings.

○

○

The heart's flame rekindle:
Hear though deaf, see though blind
Help love its object find.

○

In the bay of solitude
Surges a rip tide of deep emotion—
All, eventually, enter this ocean.

In the tricky currents
Some drown, some float, some swim
And some leave, worn thin.

○

The violinist
Plays with emotional intensity
Eyes closed.

○

The beagle chases a rabbit
Into a field of wild flowers
There losing the scent.

○

Who loves the rose
Has a heart
And a nose.

○

○

At the celebration
The victorious Spartans
Hear poems by Euripides.

Overcome
They agree not to destroy Athens
Home of this poet.

So ends
The twenty-seven-year-long
Peloponnesian war.

"The Greek Way," by Edith Hamilton.

○

The winding road
Leads to a country graveyard
And ends there.

○

The heart was pierced—
Except for that sacred place
Where the stabber lives.

○

○

Mystified by the communion
Between Mozart's music and the heart
The mind, respectfully, stands apart.

○

Reflecting in the opposing mirrors
Of Know Thyself and Accept Thyself
Different images…unify…then fade.

○

The half
That craves to be exchanged
Eats only shared joy.

○

During unfolding's journey
Come storms of derangement
And sunbeams of understanding.

○

How many doomed youths
Were melted down
To cast this war memorial?

○

○

From earth's womb
Water springs forth
And collects itself.

Immature
Nature leads it
Along the lowest paths.

Constricted
It runs rapidly
Crystal clear.

Free
It moves slowly
Laden with darkness.

Finally
Tumbling into the sea
It disperses into infinity.

○

Pine branches caress the sky
As the sky embraces the tree—
At boundaries is born Unity.

○

In the afternoon quiet
A lone black kitten
Explores the sunny meadow.

○

○

Among the remains
Of last summer's floral regiment
Appear unruly spring volunteers.

○

This catbird's song
Includes everything it has overheard
Repeated all day long.

○

The mind
Attempting to express the heart's feelings
Stops when the heart smiles.

○

Such partings persist:
Joy heightened by sadness
And sadness deepened by guilt.

○

Only after the flower dies
Are its seeds freed to sprout
And seek the sky.

○

○

Tears take form
From feelings one cannot explain
And from joy, and pain.

Drop after drop
The eyes remain blurred
Turning vision inward.

○

The faded pictures
Belie the salad days
They portray.

○

Self-interest separated all
Except the prize-winning couple
Who danced with shared joy.

○

Behind the curtain
Possibilities beget possibilities
Each appearing briefly onstage.

The audience of one
Though watching intently
Seldom applauds.

○

○

Separated—
The slender fingers of longing
Caress the past.

○

Only nostrils
And two eyes
Float above the lake's surface.

At the water's edge
A great blue heron crouches
Stalking its prey.

The heron
As the three black spots approach
Stands upright, stretching its neck.

Further approaches countered by retreats
The alligator finally reverses course—
It begins to rain heavily.

○

Seeking support
Where none can be found
Two tendrils intertwine.

○

○

Each life created
He lived with zest—
And suffered as many deaths.

○

On the eastern shore
Waves from the past
Explore the future.

In the midwest
There are no waves
And time stands still.

On the western shore
Waves from the future
Break on the present.

○

The duck escapes
Wings flapping furiously
Footprints on the water.

○

A silent breeze
Released and carried off
The wind-harp's song.

○

○

With reverential intonation
The person described becomes a saint;
Spoken otherwise, merely quaint.

○

Under increasing clouds
An encircling seawall stands
Sheltering only shifting sands.

The sun breaks through—
Blue waves flow over the seawall
Unearthing the city of youth.

○

A cool wind
Blows away the dust
Inside the empty house.

○

In the strong wind
A hawk hangs motionless
In the sky.

○

The heron swallows a fish
Whose shadow wiggles beneath it
In the water.

○

○

In the fragrant summer night
Ecstatic sounds of procreation
Mix with calls of desire.

○

The chaste flower
Unlike its pollinated sisters
Continues to bloom.

○

Rare, the love
That completely fills two hearts
And two souls.

○

Who is the more disappointed
When the repeated prayer
Goes always unanswered?

○

A thorny rose amongst weeds—
Plucked by the Master's hand
Its soul is finally validated.

○

○

Under the tree canopy
Lush, shaded swamp growth
In pervasive silence.

○

A young poet
Gave the dusty, old Italian town
Beauty—and meaning.
—
"Ravenna," written by Oscar Wilde at age 20.

○

Time bleaches positive extremes
For inclusion in the pastel mosaic
Of Acceptance.

○

In the steamy swamp
The unexpected coolness
Of large white flowers.

○

Sunset—
A fishing boat on the darkening sea
Returns empty.

○

○

On Nature's face
Its ever-changing condition is masked
By expressions of grace.

○

In vanity's reply
Come truth and jealousy
Side by side.

○

Sunlight enters the silent room
Where lives once were shared
Illuminating both past and present.

○

In the town restaurant
An elderly farm couple dines
Breaking bread with strong hands.

○

Sunrise—
From the now orange sea
Dolphins leap joyfully.

○

○

A cloud slowly drifts by
Like a long-held dream passing away
Leaving an empty, blue sky.

○

Herons calling—
Small ripples
In deep silence.

○

Young and dispassionate
Truth would be known
As old and wise.

○

Golden days
Are first named so
In reverie.

○

Her eyes
Announce the memory
Before it is described.

○

○

In the darkness
Owl eyes
Glowing.

○

Dawn—
Swans
Rising.

○

With confident eyes
The tiger invites its target
To accept death.

○

Twilight—
The Towhee's plaintive calls
Taper off.

○

Dreams
Sprout best
In hostile soil.

○

◯

In the field
Stand wild flowers of loveliness
And a stone of sorrow.

◯

His diagnosis, terminal—
He savors the day
Sitting outdoors, alone.

◯

An uneven race—
While Ripening proceeds by intermittent leaps
Time keeps a steady pace.

◯

Racing, lungs bursting
Carrying a lion's weight and wounded
The zebra collapses.

◯

Although unpollinated
The lovely, fragrant, full-blown rose
With indifference greets the bee.

◯

○

Their impassioned chords reinforcing
Two young musicians playing duets
Fall in love.

When the music ends
The audience and both performers
Maintain a long silence.

○

No blood shows
Where the tears
Ran down.

○

As the consciousness in it
Becomes conscious of it
The moment is forever transformed.

○

Holding the baby
The new grandmother
Enters the past.

○

○

The heart judges not
The conflicting feelings
It also creates.

○

Hesitantly
The swollen bud
Begins to unfold.

○

Quietly, in the moonlight
Tree-branch shadows
Sweep the garden path.

○

Finally a fragrant vision fulfilled—
Alas, the passionate embrace was crushing
And, now, two fragrances persist.

○

The old monk
For words to describe silence
Sacrifices silence.

○

○

Leaving nothing behind
Except a bud in winter quarters
The dappled leaf departs.

○

As the hawk
Carries the rabbit aloft
One last, disappearing scream.

○

The bow fully bent
And the arrow pulled to his cheek
The hunter—hesitates.

○

The understanding that arrives
Beyond the power to repair
Brings remorse and despair.

○

Yesterday
Became poignant
After death intervened.

○

○

The significance
In love's presence
Absence measures.

○

Dilemma
Thrashes on a knife edge
Bleeding.

○

The wall of silence
Casts deep shadows
On both sides.

○

This servant's strengths
Feed upon the weaknesses
Of the master.

○

Having just imagined
Life without them
The conversation deepens.

○

○

Meanings
Are summarized
On elderly faces.

○

Attacked at every step
By peers and the mighty
It marched straight ahead.

Reaching the last row
It could now become anyone
Even a king or queen.

Without hesitation
It chose to remain a pawn
Turned, and counterattacked.

○

The grieving widower
Photographs the just emptied house
Then slowly drives away.
—
For Bill Hess.

○

○

Having won the prize
The child poses with his flower arrangement
Enhancing it.

○

Every apartment
Has a short-term lease
And a different view.

Most tenants
Searching for the ideal view
Try to change apartments.

The old janitor
Familiar with all the views
Lives contentedly in the basement.

○

Rage not
Against the dying of the light
This meteor exposed the night.

○

The quiet shore
Turns back
An angry sea.

○

○

The undeserved prize
Comes wrapped
In anger.

○

Ripeness adds colors
To the limited palette
Of experience.

○

It hops—and sings:
A solitary mockingbird
Missing one wing.

○

A castle
Once captured, then abandoned
Now shelters emptiness.

○

Before falling
The dry leaves on the Bodhi tree
Rustle death poems.

○

○

Emerging from the fire
The molten mass congeals
Part lead, part gold.

○

In the silence
Separating them
The ticking of time.

○

Life drifts slowly
Through Sunday afternoon
Aware of Monday's waterfall.

○

Familiar surroundings
In an unexpected mist
Invite exploration.

○

The realities
Young imagination constructed
Ripening remodels.

○

○

On his old face
Deeply furrowed by pain
The eyes still twinkle.

○

Snow
Falls into the pond
Silently.

○

Rain
Cleansing the flower buds
Awakens one.

○

An enduring fragrance—
Every bud of potential
Blossomed in its hour.

○

Facing the rising sun
The bird sings as if this dawn
Were the very first.

○

○

Imagination
Dwells at the crossroad of perceptions
Creating realities.

With unbearable traffic
Imagination creates other realities
Devoid of perceptions.

Offering comfort
Some would clothe all such realities
In gray, confining overcoats.

Relentlessly
Imagination creates sill more realities
Requiring no such clothes.

—

For Emily Dickinson.

○

Its impending end
Renders this special day
Luminous.

○

Only those corn seeds
Reluctant to sprout
Now fatten this crow.

○

○

Hidden by smoke
From the forest fire
A rainstorm arrives.

○

With relish
Chaos also upsets
Boredom.

○

With Ripening
That beheld
Also mellows.

○

A solitary stone
Meditates in the black water
Surrounded by floating leaves.

○

One guest
Wearing somber clothing
Mainly observes.

○

○

What became significant
Was the Awareness
Behind the poem.
—

"In Sicily," by Siegfried Sassoon.

○

A stone
Thrown across the border
Aroused two armies.

○

In the chalice
Of a white lily
A bee dreams.

○

That lost
Through the broken heart
Entered it.

○

Twilight—
The Mockingbird's songs
Lengthen.

○

○

A soprano's song
Overheard one summer evening
Has still not faded.

○

Small, the boat
That carries away
A shattered dream.
—
O-Bon festival.

○

Empathy
Scrutinizes
Silences.

○

The silenced feelings
Reluctantly become the poem
Wherein reconciliation lies.

○

A cold wind stirs—
The cloud and its shadow
Quietly move away.

○

○

In the dissonance
Only the heart of the matter
Sounds a pure note.

○

Ripeness:
The mellowness of Autumn
Spiced with Spring joy;

And poetry
No longer extracted from the Moment
But, instead, put into it.

○

Part II—After Age 70

"We grow too soon old and too late smart."
—*Amish proverb*

○

Ripened at last—
The century plant
Quietly blooming.

○

A fallen flower chalice—
Its treasure of nectar and raindrops
Slowly ebbing away.

○

For once
Their souls
Converse.

○

One by one
Blossoms drifting with the ebb tide
Sink.

○

One flower chalice
Growing face downward
Thirsts for raindrops.

○

○

The child is unaware
And the grandparent doesn't explain
The burden of chronic pain.

○

Looking back—
A zigzag path
Connecting random events.

○

Contending in the same eyes
Are the glow from first love
And the detachment of Zen.

○

Returning to the old house—
Even the memories
Have changed.

○

Disturbing the surface
Of a pleasant memory
Some regret oozed forth.

○

○

Reaching toward a starry heaven
A solitary cypress stands outside the village
Separated from both.†

The barred asylum window—
Just outside, a solitary iris
In full bloom.‡

A little hope remained:
Above the ominous landscape, two white clouds;
The shot, to his stomach.*

―

† Van Gogh's painting "Starry Night" from Arles.

‡ His stunning painting in the Ottawa museum (untitled) from the asylum at St. Remy.

* His painting "Crows Over A Wheat Field" from Auvers.

○

Circling the Anhinga
The young alligator is unsure
Whether to eat or play.

○

As sunset approaches
The seemingly stable backdrop
Begins to crumble.

○

○

Picking up the letter
And reading it again
Its impact is undiminished.

○

Another
Interrupted relationship—
A different pain.

○

Around its core
Of calm and light
Swirls the hurricane's fury.

○

Heartfelt comments—
The coolness of strangers
Becomes the warmth of friends.

○

The lonely widow
Trying to make a new friend
Retells her husband's stories.

○

○

Of all pleasant memories
The unexpected kindness
Became the strongest.

○

Gold enters the bloodstream
To tempt the body
While starving the soul.

○

Muted
Are the world's drumbeats
Here in Nature's presence.

○

One nestling falls—
Its mother's song
Ceases.

Below
The unfeathered body
Answers no call.

○

○

Pure flattery—
She enjoys it
Nevertheless.

○

Preceded by evasion
And followed by acquiescence
Chaos brings change.

○

Now irrelevant
The dreams of youth are displaced
By simple pleasures.

○

Apprehension in the Mockingbird's song—
The first forecast
Of an approaching storm.

○

Migrating birds from the north
Bring this wonderful surprise in Autumn:
Familiar Spring songs.

○

○

The price
Of an inner passage
Is one ordinary life.

Who sets forth
Struggles alone
To avert disaster.

Glances and polite conversation
Become the infrequent exchanges
With the parallel world.

Encountered
Are focused longing
And spiritual joy.

Near sunset
The spiritual journey complete
The parallel paths rejoin.

Without expectations
Ordinary and extraordinary
Become one.

—

For Emily Dickinson.

○

○

Youth cries, "it's not enough"—
"That's all there is—but try,"
The elderly reply.

○

A Buddhist's face—
In the parade of conflicting persuasions
It alone is serene.

○

A sudden breeze
Lifts the tresses of Spanish moss
Revealing deeper gloom beyond.

○

Traveling south
He discovered the Provence
He brought with him.

○

A mockingbird sings—
Startled, it flies away
Still singing.

○

○

No light can enter
Because of the raging storm
Within.

○

Ignoring his own shortcomings
His children learned
And returned them.

○

Exchanging warm smiles
Two strangers pass each other—
Their fantasies promising, both turn.

○

Snails' trails—
One nocturnal food search
Ended abruptly.

○

The leaves
In the silence of isolation
Also sigh.

○

○

Helping them survive
I saw a future
That is now unfolding.

○

Let go—
Nothing worthwhile falls away
And that lost, insight replaces.

○

A fragrance
From flowering honeysuckle
Displaces every thought.

○

The mockingbird
Brings to its caged offspring
Poison berries.

○

Autumn—
In this season of decline
Ripening awakens.

○

○

The shaded plaque
Became illuminated by the setting sun
Revealing names deprived of dreams.
—
Plaque at Brasenose College, Oxford, in memory of its students who died in the British and German armies during World War I.

○

A dry leaf
Loosened by this gentle breeze
Drifts away.

○

Cut down
The Allamandas spring back
Yellow trumpets blazing.

○

The Pruner's wand
Reveals both age and beauty
In the neglected garden.

○

Above
The gloom
A sunlit branch.

○

○

This bleak land
Once farmed with little success
Is again at peace.

Some of the pain
From the failed effort
Remains with the ruins.

○

A rare stone arrowhead—
Shaped for death
And for beauty.
—
The Native American Clovis arrowhead.

○

Influences never suspected
In early memories
Are revealed at sunset.

○

Humor and paradox
He breathed into subjects
Enlarging their souls.
—
For Oscar Wilde.

○

○

The crows' lookout
Failing to report the fox
Is silenced by the flock.

○

Divining its significance
Is the last hurdle
Before the journey ends.

○

One shadow
Became
An alligator.

○

The shadows of yesterday
Delay the dawning
Of today.

○

With ripening
The senses terminate
In the heart.

○

○

Emptied, it simply reflects;
Its response sounds hollow;
And it cannot be refilled.

This Emptiness
Has an aura
And a resonance.

○

The touch most keenly felt
Comes from the parallel world
Which cannot be touched.

○

The Towhee's only melody
Is sung cheerfully all day
But wistfully at twilight.

○

He planted a Hawthorn tree
And anxiously awaited the blossoms—
He was not to see.
—
For Ken Siegel.

○

○

Hardly anyone notices
The wide-open door—
Guarded, it intrigues all.

○

Noon—
The old bridge only supports sunshine
And some trailing vines.

○

As more mills close
Fewer trains pass by—
On rails now rusting.

○

Mozart arias—
Birds, too, are listening
Intently.

○

Ripened empathy
Becomes eager to help
And move on.

○

○

The young mockingbird
Sings perfectly
Its ancient song.

The older mockingbird
Also sings perfectly
Its neighbors' songs.

○

The fallen yellow trumpets
Still awaiting the call to sound
Lie silent upon the ground.

○

Continued neglect
Starved the possibility
Of love.

○

The deep mine
Gives up gold dust first
And nuggets last.

○

○

Feelings
That touched her heart
Live now in other homes.

○

At the crossroads
A Prophet foretells the consequences
Then leaves—unheeded.

○

The silent part
Of her answer
Contains its meaning.

○

Clouded sunrise—
The mockingbird's entire repertoire
Elicits no dawn chorus.

○

In the pervasive silence
The canal and its towpath
Lead to the horizon.

○

○

Atop the mountain of Loneliness
He could best describe the valley
And the heavens.
—
For Thoreau.

○

The influential few
Conspired to have a bugle blown
And the young came running.

In the shaded valley
Between two mountains of corpses
A surrender took place.

○

A Viking-Prophet amalgam:
The Prophet restrains the Viking
Who encourages the Prophet.

○

That day's end
Wrapped itself around them
And wouldn't let go.
—
Last meeting of Mom and J.P.

○

○

The final transition—
The spirit crosses the barrier
Inviting the body to follow.

Mozart's "Requiem"
Describes his unique bridge
The final "amen" its keystone.

Van Gogh's last painting[†]
Portrays his impassible barrier—
Necessitating other means for crossing.

Emily Dickinson
Intuiting the barrier early
Never needed to cross it.

———

[†] "Crows Over A Wheat Field," from Auvers.

○

Approached now
The horizon
No longer recedes.

○

About the Author

J. C. Greene spent much of his working life designing radio astronomy and telecommunications systems, and founding and managing Comtech Laboratories. Including an interval of military service, he also "found" time to raise a family and pursue enduring interests, such as liberal arts, music, gardening, economics, Japanese arts, and especially Haiku poetry.

For further information, or to contact the author, visit http://www.opengatehaiku.com.

978-0-595-40895-5
0-595-40895-8

Printed in the United States
71493LV00002B/346-399

9 780595 408955